A Safe and Brave Space
Anthology of Poetry and Art

Volume 2

by

Garden Sisters of the Garden of Neuro

Published by Garden of Neuro Publishing
Poughkeepsie, New York
Copyright © A Safe and Brave Space
November 2022

Library of Congress Control Number:

ISBN 979-8-9851332-2-6 Paperback

Internal Art Director: Pratibha Savani
Publishing Consultant: Lisa Tomey-Zonneveld, Manager Prolific Pulse Press LLC
Cover Art by: Ana Stjelja
Cover Design by: Pratibha Savani
Edited by: Garden of Neuro Ambassadors
Internal Art: Garden of Neuro Members

Table of Contents

Ana Stjelja...1

  WHAT THE LEAF HIDES?..1

Barbara Simmons...2

Chyrel J. Jackson 5

Danielle Martin 6

  You Are...6

Karen Monteith..10

  Forest Peace 10

Kathy Jo Bryant...13

  My Best Place to Be...13

  Safe and Brave Space 14

Lauren Salkin...17

  Cocoa Comfort 17

Lea Ervin..18

  Summit..18

Lin Marshall Brummels..21

  Unwanted Beauty 21

  Home Early or Not at All 22

  It's Not the End 23

Lisa Tomey-Zonneveld...24

  Where you lead, you also follow..24

  When You Can 27

Mary Anne Zammit 28

  The girl at the Second Floor 28

  Buddhist Sun 29

  Stories in the Wind..30

Nanci Arvizu 33

Safe, Brave, Space..33

Safety Questions..34

Paula Frew 37

My Cave..37

Remember Her 38

Pratibha Savani 39

Dreams 39

In Comfort..40

Richa Dinesh Sharma... 43

Unfurl..43

Self-Reflection..44

Robin Klammer 47

Washed Away..47

Susan Brearley 48

Traveling the Muddy Roads 48

Tina Hudak... 51

AS I AGE 51

Vanessa Caraveo 52

The Haven Within Me..52

A Haven Full of Light..53

Yasmin S Brown 54

I Want to Feel Free..54

Zaneta Varnado Johns 57

In No Rush 57

My Home, My Refuge..58

Contributing Artists & Authors..61

Acknowledgements

We would like to acknowledge the following for their contributions to this publication:

Pratibha Savani, author of *Tangles + Knots*, for inspiring us to use black and white art for mindfulness colouring, in this anthology. And for editing the art contributions to this publication.

Cover Artist Ana Stjelja

Cover Designer Pratibha Savani

To all the editors who volunteered their time to make this anthology shine, namely Nanci Arvizu, Susan Brearley, Pratibha Savani, Lisa Tomey-Zonneveld.

For Workshop facilitators Pratibha Savani and Lisa Tomey-Zonneveld.

Dedication

This poetry anthology, now reaching Volume 2, comes from the women's collective that is found in the Garden of Neuro, and is dedicated to all the women who nourished it, so that it could grow into what you hold in your hands. With grateful hearts for what we have birthed together, we share this with you dear reader, and invite you to be a part of this wonderful experiment that we have begun--a global women's community honoring our differences as well as our shared experiences--for the benefit of all of us.

A Safe and Brave Space

Gathered around the table
To dream, to write, to share
Women nurtured by love
For one another
Grew and took their words
Into their care and blossomed
Poetry, pictures, prose
Like a bouquet of flowers
Each bloom is special
Purpose is powerful
Praise is possible
Strength is inevitable
When women come to the table
Ideas grow, dreams are known
Life gets better
In a safe and brave space

Lisa Tomey-Zonneveld
Garden of Neuro Poet Laureate, 2022-2023

Safe and Brave Art Space

All artwork contributed by the
Garden of Neuro Ambassadors

Welcome to volume 2 of our safe
and brave art space. We continue the
interactive element of black and white
mindfulness art within this anthology.

Our garden artists creatively took to the
brief, which was presented in our bespoke
online art workshop, and they created
exquisite versions of their safe and brave
spaces, giving you another beautiful
expressive experience of poetry and
mindfulness art to indulge in.

Find a quiet place
Indulge in peace
Submerge in patterns
Colour where they meet

Art & Intro by Pratibha Savani

Art by Pratibha Savani

Ana Stjelja

WHAT THE LEAF HIDES?

What the leaf hides

Is a seductive dance

Of a lady dressed in autumn

An unknown heroine

Of the war for yellow Love

And brown Hope.

This leaf has fallen

From the tree of Wonders

In the rhythm of a symphony

So beautiful and divine

She dances in the middle of

The enchanted forest.

What the leaf hides?

Barbara Simmons

Sweeping, not swept away
(Inspired by "Hella Feminism" at the Oakland Museum of Art)

I view her broom, her dustpan, her feather duster,
accessories for the times
when women cleaned up, tidied up,
made sure the world was free
from dust, from dirty laundry piling up,
when women of the house did not have time to think about,
should not have time to think about,
complications beyond domestic borders.
Laden with the tools she'll need,
Ms. Clingfree wears, along with her supplies,
her disdain for the stage she stands upon:
oh yes, I'll clean and scrub and straighten out for you,
and still remain your object of desire,
and when all is swept away, I suppose I'm supposed
to let you sweep me off my tired feet.
Who's in her mirror, who's center of this private stage,
when she is often in the wings?
Who do I see right now, the me in my mirror,
a woman with more pens than scrubbing brushes,
a woman who's learned how to be alone and feel 'with',
a woman who's swept the pressed and ironed myths
away, replacing them with all that's true, and fair, and
wrinkled.

Art by Pratibha Savani

What makes me feel safe is...

_____

_____

_____

_____

_____

_____

_____

_____

_____

_____

Chyrel J. Jackson

Forgotten Songs of the Ancestors

Mary and Martha have every reason to weep and moan…
Black souls have borne witness to the following atrocities on
North American shores:
The Auction blocks of Jamestown paraded my raped and
mutilated children.
Founding fathers' Southern Slave plantations and cotton
fields,
Jim Crow,
Segregation,
Night rides of the Ku Klux Klan,
Selma Alabama,
Church Bombings,
Bloody Sunday and Edmund Pettus Bridge.
Tulsa Oklahoma-Black Wallstreet,
Lynchings and unarmed civilian shootings at the hands of
white police.
Civil rights, and voting rights violations,
White washing of Black History and Black Literature,
Book Bans,
Corrupt politicians,
Least in wealth doubled in illness
Tripled in violence and death.
My weary Black soul has long forgotten the comforting lulls
of the ancestors.
I lie awake at 4:40 a.m. with full knowledge there is no safe
space for Black women/people
there simply never was.
Not on this blood-soaked soil.
So tired of singing slave master songs,
will I ever break free of founding fathers' wrongs???

Danielle Martin

You Are

When your shadow paints my insecurities to match
so that we are at the same stage in life,
when fingers weave together as if by magic
and time no longer holds,
when words do not venture further than thoughts,
and I'm welcomed into your embrace
under the knowing moonlight
while rolling through country trails,
that is my safe space.
Or when partially submerged in aqua waves
while sunrays sketch portraits on open backs
that is my brave space.
Against leaning coconut trees, bodies tied in wisps of thin cool threads
fed by the buzzing tropical breeze.
No matter the place, or time of day
it's always the same when you're near
for you are my safe and brave space.

"Belief"
Art by Danielle Martin

I feel most courageous when...

_____
_____
_____
_____
_____
_____
_____
_____
_____
_____
_____
_____
_____
_____
_____
_____
_____
_____

Within

Children once played in open parks
touching grass and public water taps.
Sharing snacks piece by piece
wiping tiny fingers all over the place,
while laughing all day through.

They sneezed and coughed holding each other tight
under the watchful eyes of parents gathered nearby.

They learned so much, through touch, taste and smell.
Sights and sounds livening up their sphere.
Then they grew to live adult lives either near or far
forging new safe and brave spaces
in a world, froth with dichotomy of being.

But today, these same spaces have changed, turning grey.
Smiles no longer beam bright,
touching kills and keeping one's distance is the new outdoor game.
Wipes, hand sanitizer and temperature monitors the wardens of health
and hugs are rare
for no space is safe and the only brave space lies within.

Karen Monteith

the understory
combined with overstory
create safe haven

Forest Peace

Meandering the forest, I discover a peaceful calm where I can think, be brave, and be a child again. Overstory arms cast a blanket over myself and its understory. Its uniqueness is continually balanced with seasonal changes. I courageously wander alone, with my thoughts as companions, among the trees, flora, berries, and emerging buds. There are those creatures big and small, watching me, who I do not see. I marvel in wonder at nature's magnificence. I gasp to refresh myself to fit back into society and what needs to be done. Tomorrow, I will return to these same trails where the peaceful calm cloaks me.

Art by Karen Monteith

Things that make me Happy

_____
_____
_____
_____
_____
_____
_____
_____
_____
_____
_____
_____
_____
_____
_____
_____
_____

Kathy Jo Bryant

My Best Place to Be

A place where I can feel at home
A space which I can call my own
A corner of a comfort zone
A lot of love that's to me shown

A time when loved ones hug, embrace
And hold us close, yes, face to face
A feeling, sweet, of peace and grace
An open feeling and where one prays

This is just where I love to be
This is where I'll have bravery
This place will have no slavery
This place will be so safe for me!

Safe and Brave Space

Let Me Be Me
O, let me be who I need to be
With a place for my true identity

A chance to develop and to grow
A woman who spreads her love, just so

A place to sprinkle blessings around
And help those with dark troubles, bound

For I love helping those who need
To fill a vacant place with a tiny seed

A seed of love to share with those
Who need a life like the sun which glows

So please let me be who I need to be
And cover the world with love, like the sea!

Art by Kathy Jo Bryant

My garden grows best when...

Lauren Salkin

Cocoa Comfort

Where sadness never weeps
Sweet silky treat
heartbeat quickening, fix of simplicity
conjuring precious adolescent memories
flickering at twilight in a darkening sky
Abandoned spaces drift in clouds
below shuttered doors hide rainbows
from clattering footfalls
In the hall, a man child shouts, his words
echoing as he pounds the walls
In a time once before, but now she is safe
in a color-coated sky fear cedes to peace
where sadness never weeps
except in darkness beneath
A child tosses in her sleep
waiting for shadows to follow
footsteps behind locked doors
In a time once before, but now she is safe
inside a quiet mind, thoughts float
in a place where a child never cries
She remembers sipping cocoa

Lea Ervin

Summit

Bricks are laid stacks on stacks
Red, brown, and black.
I open the doors; the heals of my boots clack
Echoing hellos as I move my way back.
To the left and to the right
To find respite in the familiar place
I lived before.
The hallway mile, the aqua tile
Jesus on the Cross gazing at me.
Paneled walls warm the hall
To the rose garden room where she died.
If I so I ever fret, worry, or pine
My mind takes me back to the brick house on Summit
High on the hill that smelled of pine.

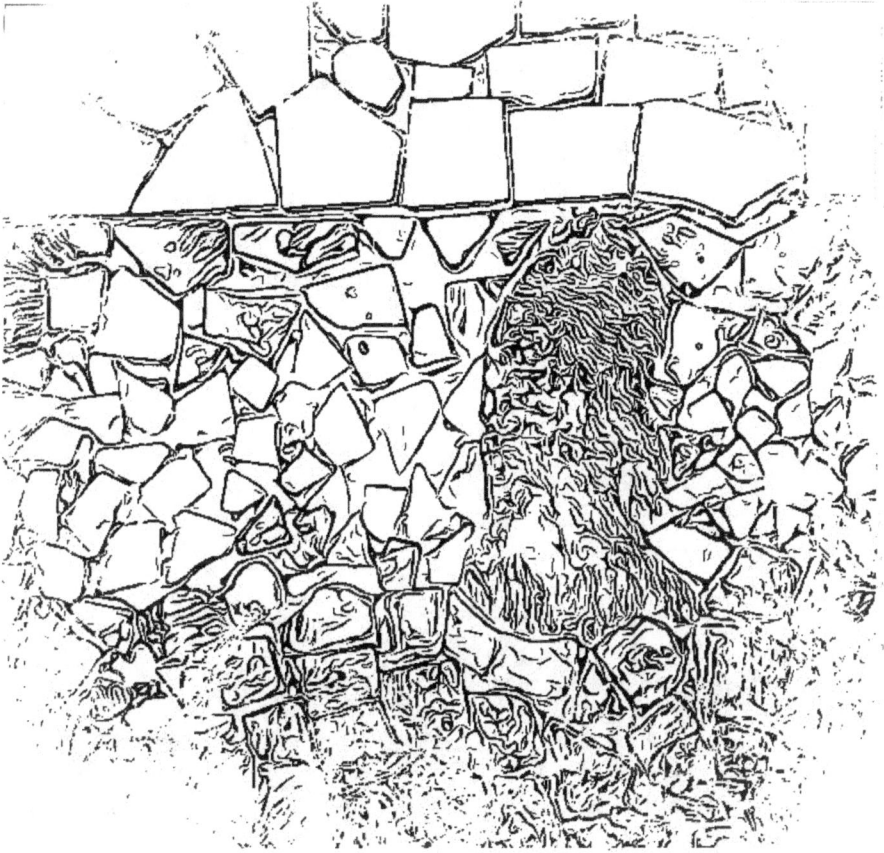

"Meditation"
Art by Danielle Martin

*I can create a
safe haven by...*

Lin Marshall Brummels

Unwanted Beauty

We rarely see beauty in ourselves
but occasionally someone sees it in us.
In nature, Canadian, bull, and musk
thistles are unwanted beauties.
They are declared noxious by Weed Boards
that look over fields, send landowners
warning notices to clean up, and if weeds
are not removed on time, levy big fines.
Thistles produce lovely purple flowers
that mature into fluff-covered ripe seeds.
One must snip carefully, pile cottony
seed heads together in a bag and remove
before they blow with summer's
furnace winds across vast grasslands,
dispersing noxious weed seeds
viable for fifty years. It's my fervent hope
we clear our personal toxic weeds
in fewer years. Plant seeds of change,
feel the beauty that's been there all along.

Home Early or Not at All

I wasn't meant for waiting and wondering, Gus, she said.
Larry McMurtry from *Comanche Moon*

He'll be home early or not at all
It's Saturday night, time to howl
Squealing tires on his tired El Camino
He flees the domestic scene – oh.
She goes to find a friendly face
at Smoky Samz, the local bar,
wants to improve the night's pace
but hasn't done well alone so far.
Another meal at the kitchen table
strikes her as one more fable
sold to women to keep them happy
while their men treat them crappy.
He returns somber and contrite.
She stays out all the next night,
puts on a brave new morning face,
knows it's time for a safer place.

It's Not the End

Warm winter days
invite spring dreams

Sticky cinnamon rolls
are best when warm -
sip hot coffee or tea,
wash sugar away

Chewing fingernails
is a sign of distress -
see a counselor,
unburden you mind

Think out-of-the-box,
smile often -
every soul deserves
a happy ending

If you aren't happy,
it's not the end

Lisa Tomey-Zonneveld

Where you lead, you also follow

imagine you are seated
at a table of representatives
they have their agendas
you have yours

what resolutions are found
may come with cooperation
with proposed risks
with open minds

when we take a stand
when we find courage
to share our heart in full
chances are we will find answers

if we do not
then we risk a stand not affirmed
a dream unfulfilled
a loss unresolved

celebrate your differences
take a stand for what is right
risk a belief in the good
stand strong with all your might

Art by Lisa Tomey-Zonneveld

Doodles

When You Can

with the world in its condition
I feel responsible to fulfill my own mission
when hearts bleed upon my shoes
my desire to speak up kicks in
what matters is to take a stand
be a beacon for our fellow citizens
this takes courage when others find
degradation, for simply being
a certain color, a certain belief
completely deserving of equal life
then I ask myself
what about the courage it takes
for my friends to walk down a street
just to wear a hoodie, buy some gum
when they reach to their pockets
to pay for something
because they are people of color
assumptions are up and they are put down
where is my courage then
where do we go from here

Mary Anne Zammit

The girl at the Second Floor

She goes out smiling.

Full make up, high heels.

She walks hand in hand with her beloved.

She is the girl in the second floor.

Furnished flat, luxury.

Some even envy her, for her life, for the dream.

Door closes.

And when she removes her make up, there are scars and lines of tears.

She will never let you see.

Then one day, she escapes from her cage and she will show the world

The true reality of the second floor.

Buddhist Sun

The Sun,

shines on my face.

Under skies more like crystals.

The Sun,

warms cold valleys after winter.

I attempt to gaze up and let the sun take me away from the lonely corners of my thoughts.

Buddhist Sun,

diverts me to the ocean of silence.

Not one single thought.

Because I am now a bird.

Stories in the Wind

Last night you broke my bracelet.

The one sealed on the bridge of eternal love.

The wind.

Told me everything.

But before you called out my name.

Sealed on the Sun, my eternal

Carved on sands

And the days when you burned me

Like a witch.

Like a doll.

I heard your voice in the songs of the stars,

You were moaning, longing for me to fall for your eyes.

I loved them and wrote lines of waves.

I only wish the deserts sands to take you away

I know if you call me again.

I come to you.

To death.

When the day is shining.

Skies are clear.

It is hard to die.

Art by Lisa Tomey-Zonneveld

My home is...

Nanci Arvizu

Safe, Brave, Space

Safe is
To be included, welcomed, comfortable,
sheltered, fed, clothed
To be heard, happy, excited
allowed, free, vivacious
To be conscious, aware, enlightened
curious, outrageous, me

The wish to be brave
requires situations
to prove it
Be always ready
observant with your actions
and kind with your words

I create space to feel vibration
In its purest form
where wisdom passes
to a seeking student
Where my heart is held
and moments
are cherished forever

Safety Questions

How does one learn the feeling of safety when nowhere is safe?
Where is safety in numbers when the numbers turn against you?

Do we learn to be comfortable in the false safety surrounding us from birth?
And when we find ourselves back inside the very thing we have been trying to escape, how can we trust the hand of help?

Finding a voice, the ability to calm the trigger finger pulling at raw emotions, a whisper roaring into a monstrous wind.

And what will my voice say, if I were to hold back the screams long enough to hear the words of the broken parts inside me? Will my words heal this wound equally? Finally? Forever?

Words that must be shared like bricks in the path laid down to give the next one a place to plant her feet as her soul sings to the wind.

"What's on My Mind"
Art by Nanci Arvizu

I am grateful for...

_____
_____
_____
_____
_____
_____
_____
_____
_____
_____
_____
_____
_____
_____
_____
_____
_____
_____
_____
_____
_____
_____

Paula Frew

My Cave

It was dark and filled with
the unknown.
I explored
despite rumors I had heard; I saw
no monsters, no ghosts.
I searched books
to populate
my cave.
After hauling
my books,
there I sat
and read with
my flashlight.
One day, the
cave was beguiling, and I
closed my eyes and slept.
I awoke to yells of
worry and of threat.
I decided to be brave and venture out
to accept my punishment.
Mother yelled,
"Is that where you have been all this time? Under The bed?"
I looked back and sure enough,
my cave became my bed.
I would return many days to
read, but the magic was
gone.

Remember Her

After Joy Harjo

Remember her who was nestled
snug in your arms.
Remember her who was secure enough
to communicate
to you.
Remember her who was safe to
love you because you loved
her, too.
Remember her who you forsook,
no longer safe to speak,
to love.
Remember her who was brave enough
to love you and brave enough to
love again.

Pratibha Savani

Dreams

Reality submerges with fiction
As I leap from this world
Into the dreamworld
My existence is real
But my dreams are not
But my subconscious
Thinks it's real
So that's enough

I know what I feel
As I wake up
That was unreal
As my dreams
Are filled up
So refreshing
It unravels
As I try to recall
Dreaming is my solitude
For my body and soul

In Comfort

In the comfort
Of these four walls
Lay my salvation
Away from everything else
To do what I wish
To create what I want
To sit where I choose
To watch what I want
The only living space
Where every room is available
Every vision is mine
Every spot I turned to
Every space I enter
Devours me in its sereneness
Embellished in the colours
I have chosen
To entertain in
To live in
To be in
What I call
Home

"Dream Cloud"
Art by Pratibha Savani

Richa Dinesh Sharma

Unfurl

Careful! The edges might bleed
into a callous sheet
unfurl with care, my dears,
my thoughts, please, pay heed!
I am beginning to see your forms,
your lines and where they lead
your concentricness so neat
so happy to be in a loop, on repeat
such is how you soothe yourself
in floral patterns, geometrical philosophy
of motion, expanding ever outwards
till you touch some other soul
that needs a share in your peace
So, I sit with you several times
in a day, month, or a year
just to soak in your whiteness
to feel absolved in the dark lines
I unfurl in petals that increase
as I rebuild the strength I had
as I breathe free of myself
into an infinity of possibilities
I begin to extrapolate…

Self-Reflection

Such is the way of being
To see the harshest lines and
the ugliest bulges and girths
the unseemly curves and dents
and the most repugnant parts
It never comes easy, to like oneself
The sadness seems to win, then
who do we ask for help?
As we look down upon ourselves,
we miss so much, so soon
the details of our little lives
like an intricate design
etched clearly on a weathered mind,
our budding transformations
that we conceal in fear
in the shame that shields our eyes
So, in moments of utter despair
take a pause to look inside
and see the beauty you cultured
in parts, pieces, in hopes and dreams
Remember often to visit this space
However ordinary it seems to you
this glorious marvel is your life…

"Self-Reflection"
Art by Richa Dinesh Sharma

Doodles

Robin Klammer

Washed Away

I am the tidal wave
washing you away with
doubt, fear and turmoil

You flail about,
Scared to be sucked
into the undertow of defeat.
Fear paralyses you.

I am the undercurrent,
threatening to pull you under.
You become fatigued;
Survive or surrender?

The safety of shore beckons you.
Are you brave enough to hold on?

Or will you succumb,
to the depths of my ocean floor?

You must find your innate will
to not only survive but also thrive!

Susan Brearley

Traveling the Muddy Roads

Sure. I can smile and laugh now. That is not what life always
looked like.

Fact is, if I sit and think too hard, I remember all the muddy
roads.

The places where my shoes got stuck and I had to lift my feet
out
Leave my shoes behind and continue on, barefoot.

Toes digging down deep in that mud
while my heartbeat sped up
Not knowing what the bottoms of my feet might touch.
What my toes might wiggle into.

Somewhere, deep in my insides, so deep I could feel the
butterfly nerves

I reach inside myself with my own invisible hands and touch
those vibrating wings of the monarchs
all clustered together on the tree of my spine.

And find the courage to take one more step
And one more.
And risking everything
I start to run. I start to fly.

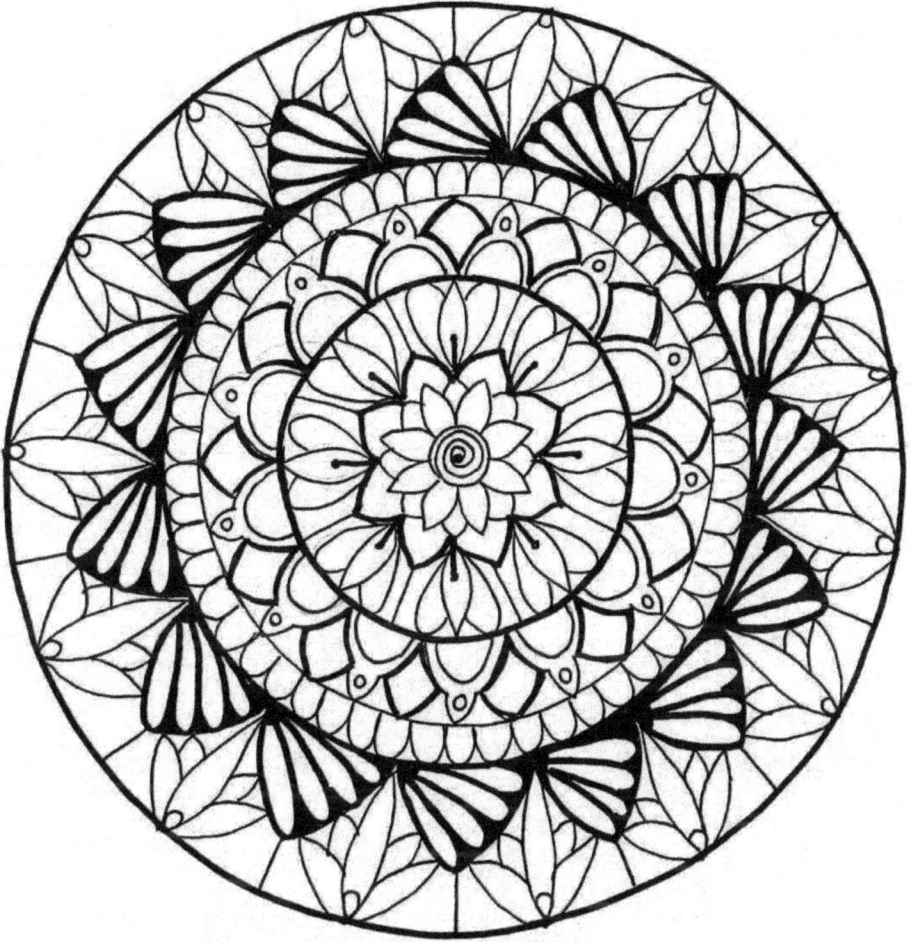

"Unfurl"

Art by Richa Dinesh Sharma

Doodles

Tina Hudak

AS I AGE

As I age, I would like to sit across from my mother
at our kitchen table, the one with the red and stripes glaring
against the hard, white enamel top, where she rolled out
her dough for our Christmas panettone, year after year.
The one where she set countless hot meals before us,
except Sunday when my father made spaghetti for her.

I would like to talk with her, mother to daughter,
about our families, our marriages, and her grandsons.
My boys. I would like to know my enigmatic father through
her eyes. Through her heart; to laugh at tales of my sisters as
toddlers, born long before me, all living in my Zia Clara's
upstairs apartment on the wrong side of town.
On the South side. The immigrants' side.

There is so much I ache for, but mostly it is this:
to have my mother close by me again, with her smiles and
scowls in equal measures; the sound of her voice carrying the
cadence and inflections of her first language. All this
surrounding me. Simply to be in her presence,
sharing our lives, as women do.

Vanessa Caraveo

The Haven Within Me

A safe and brave space I have found
to share my talents with the world
and no longer worry of feeling judged
or ridiculed for my unique thoughts and ideas.
Gone are the days I was the slave of
what closed-minded people thought about me
and where each critique injured me
like a dove with a hurt wing who is
unable to fly to the heights it was destined for.

Now I fly without fear and full of confidence
for I have found this beautiful haven
where others have also had the valiance
to spread their wings and become messengers
sharing their voice and making a difference
in this chaotic yet beautiful world we live in.

We must all look within ourselves
and learn to be our authentic selves
knowing this will help us live our true purpose
and reach our highest self who we were destined to be.
With time the long and challenging journey showed me
That safe and brave haven was inside of me all along
and now I inspire to help others find that haven
within themselves and prosper in life.

A Haven Full of Light

I was lost for so long unable to find
the light at the end of the tunnel I was in.
I thought I could keep it all inside me
yet I felt the anguish growing more and more
each day without an outlet that was desperately
needed. Too embarrassed to ask for help I
continued in the darkness without any hope.

That was until one day, someone reached out their
hand to me and told me to confide and trust,
that I was no longer alone. I was wary at first
but felt there was no other cure for all of my
despair and so I did. Little by little my world
began to be transformed by light and
my eyes no longer saw a black hole
of darkness but rather a new bright road full
of new opportunities and much abundance.

Today, I let others know they are not alone
and to be afraid to open themselves up and trust.
There are good people in this world and who
can share their own light that will help illuminate
any dark roads we are currently in. Know there
are safe and brave havens that exist and are
waiting for their doors to be opened if we
allow them to be so we can shine as we are meant to.

Yasmin S Brown

I Want to Feel Free

I purposely sit next to a tree to take in the scenery
The softness of the grass, warmness from the sun,
The radiant beauty of the flowers… I can sit here for hours
My safe space where I can close my eyes under the great big
sky.

Like the butterflies fluttering around me.
Freely acting in tune with my heartbeat, I am free.
I breathe a sigh of relief with confidence and bravery, I am
free.

Claiming a place of security
I take refuge underneath the tree without judgement.
So full of life and free…To grow and
develop everything that is inside of me, I am free.

I optimize my optimism, so the world allows me too just be
free
I feel safe and brave to just love me… I am free.
Courageous… motivated… never irresponsible…I want to be
free.

I am only responsible for my peace
I sit here covered by the tree's protective branches
Only here—on this day—do I find peace
Only here, am I safe… only here do I feel free.

"Mosaic Space"
Art by Danielle Martin

self
reflections

Things I do to process my feelings

Things that keep me busy

Things that make me feel confident

Zaneta Varnado Johns

In No Rush

I am in no rush—no hurry whatsoever
Tomorrow can take its time
Arrive whenever it pleases
This moment is mine
       to relish, or not to relish
       to share, or not to share
My choice, my prerogative

Turtles pace almost motionless
over the landscape
Not bothered by the gazelle
sprinting across Africa's Serengeti
Not bothered by man or snail
nor by other turtles
Imagine life as a turtle—carefree
Imagine their close tie with Mother Earth
Imagine their hard shell of protection
Imagine their perpetual sense of safety
Imagine being the ruler of your own time
Imagine feeling brave, safe, and in no rush!

My Home, My Refuge

Home is an open-door, arms wide-open
Familiar voices, approving eyes, fresh air
No airs, no judgement—just bare truth
Bare feet up, guards down, absolute ease
A circle of everything I love
A love of everything that encircles me
Home is good food
The sound of music—or silence
Room to dance—or just to be

Home is warmth on the coldest days
Refreshing coolness to defeat the heat
A soft landing when I'm spent
Pillows of comfort for my muse
No facade—only love behind these closed doors
Home is precious memories
A breeding place to create more
Home is a house of prayers and hope for others
My balance is here—I am centered
I have no fear—I trust entirely
My home—my refuge—fosters my well-being

Art by Lisa Tomey-Zonneveld

If I could travel anywhere I would go to...

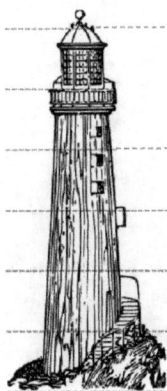

Contributing Artists & Authors

Ana Stjelja (1982, Belgrade, Serbia). In 2012 she obtained PhD (on the life and work of the Serbian woman writer Jelena J. Dimitrijević). She is a poet, writer, translator, journalist, researcher and editor. She published more than 30 books of different literary genres. In 2018 she established the Association Alia Mundi for promoting cultural diversity.

Barbara Simmons, a Bostonian and Californian, says both coasts inspire her. An alumna of Wellesley and Johns Hopkins' Writing Seminars, and a retired educator, she savors life, envisions, celebrates, and understands with words. Some publications: *Boston Accent, NewVerse News, Soul-Lit, Capsule Stories 2022*: Swimming, and her book, *Offertories: Exclamations and Disequilibriums*.

Chyrel J. Jackson grew up in a Southern Suburb of Chicago, IL. Influenced by amazing Black writers like James Baldwin, Toni Morrison, Langston Hughes, and Sonia Sanchez. Along with her sister, Lyris D. Wallace, they published Mirrored Images and *Different Sides of the Same Coin*, modern collections of poetry.
You can find her on Sistersrocnrhyme.com

Danielle Martin is a former Caribbean Journalist and Copywriter. She is the poet behind the anthology, *Kissing Shadows: Caribbean Love poems*. As well as the author of *Sweet Talk: Caribbean Culture*. Ms. Martin's work also appears in several anthologies and online publications. Her books are currently available on Amazon.

Karen E. Monteith Karen lives, writes, reads, does needlework and enjoys her family in Barrie, Ontario, Canada. Karen is writing two books, a cookbook requested by family and a book about the healing benefit of the needle arts. You can find her writing at medium.com/@karenemonteith or on her blog at karenmonteith.com

Kathy Jo Bryant hails from Missouri, USA. She is the author of*: Golden Glowing Mushroom, Favorite Things in My World, Matchless Mosaic*. Her work is in a growing number of published anthologies. She is a member of, and former moderator for, the growing Facebook poetry group: "The Passion of Poetry"

Lauren Salkin Dysfunctional, wife, mother, and loser of stuff. Making sense out of chaos.

Writer of humor, satire, poetry, and thought pieces. Published work has appeared online and in print. *Huffington Post, Extra Newsfeed, Literally Literary, Muddyum, The Haven*, as well as *ByLine*, and *Shroud Magazine*. https://medium.com/@laurensalkin

Lea Ervin is a writer, poet, artists and writing instructor from Alabama. She holds a B.A. in English from Harding University and a M.A. in Professional and Technical Writing from the University of Arkansas-Little Rock. Lea lives in Oneonta, Alabama where her husband Brad White, and their Beagle-mix, Starla Belle.

Lin Marshall Brummels earned a BA from the University of Nebraska-Lincoln and a MS from Syracuse University. She's published poems in journals, magazines, and anthologies. Her poetry chapbooks are *Cottonwood Strong* and *Hard Times,* a 2016 Nebraska Book Award winner. Her full-length collection, *A Quilted Landscape*, was published in 2021.

Lisa Tomey-Zonneveld is Poet Laureate & Gold Ambassador of Garden of Neuro Institute. When she's not writing her next poem or creating art, she manages Prolific Pulse Press LLC, edits for *Fine Lines Literary Journal* and is a co-organizer for Living Poetry. She also teaches poetry in the Garden.

Mary Anne Zammit is a graduate from the University of Malta in Diploma in Applied Social Studies (Social Work), Diploma in Diplomatic Studies, Masters in Probation Services and in Freelance and Feature Writing. She is an author of four novels in Maltese and two in English. Her poetry has been featured in international magazines and anthologics, along with her art.

Nanci Arvizu is an author, speaker, podcaster, and tech lover with nomadic dreams. Poetry and essays published in *A Safe and Brave Space* (2021), *Fine Lines Journal* (2021), *Social Justice Inks* (2022), *Speak Magazine* (2022) and *Caring for Souls* (2022). Fiction & non-fiction e-books are available on Amazon.

Paula Frew An Ohio native, the author wrote her first poem in the fourth grade. It was entitled Daffodils. At that time, she fell in love with the form. She wrote through the angst of adolescence and into the beauties and dissonance of adulthood. She has of late begun to write flash fiction. It speaks to her as another short form. Her first chapbook, Lyrical Legacy, was published in 2021. She has also been included in several anthologies. All are available on Amazon

Pratibha Savani is a UK Poet, Artist and author of *Tangles + Knots*. Published in *Open Door Magazine* and in several anthologies, she is a creative soul, inspired by the cosmos, nature and spirituality. Pratibha likes to defy the rules with her inventive expressions on instagram and facebook as Pratibha Poetry Art.

Robin Klammer: Forlorn Canadian in a foreign land. Just give her a stack of books, good coffee & sustenance, she's good to go! Avid bookworm for life! Writer on Medium, and contributor to several publications including poetry anthologies. Dark humor is her go-to in life.

Richa Dinesh Sharma lives in Singapore with her husband, two human children and one furchild. Her poems and blogs have appeared in *FineLines* quarterly issues, *OpenDoor Poetry magazine, Our Poetry Archives, MockingHeart Review, Sweetycat Press, Ravens Quoth Press* and several anthologies. Working as a remote editor for the *FineLines Literary magazine*, she has been invited to read her works widely including The Festival of Words event, recently. Her undying love for learning extends to languages, French being her current muse. When not writing or daydreaming, she runs by the beach.

Susan Brearley is an editor, writer and poet, and writes haiku daily, teaching haiku poetry writing at Innisfree Garden, one of the world's top 10 gardens of the world. Her poetry is published on Medium.com. Most of her sunny days are spent walking and sailing through the rivers and woods of the beautiful mid-Hudson Valley, New York. Insta: gardenofneuro

Tina Hudak, born and raised in a Pennsylvania steel town, moved to D.C. in 1975. Working as an artist/writer, and school librarian while raising a family, her artist's books are included in the Library of Congress, The Harvard Art Library, and other collections. She lives a quiet life with her husband and two cats in an old farmhouse while creating visual art and writing.

Vanessa Caraveo is an award-winning author, published poet, and artist whose literary work brings focus to various social issues that exist today. She has been published in *Literature Today Journal, The Poet Magazine, Latinidad Magazine, Poetrybay, Anacua Literary Arts Review,* and in multiple anthologies throughout the years.

Yasmin S Brown is a healthcare professional with a passion for understanding people. Yasmin's core focus is women's mental health and wellness. With literacy, public speaking, and self-expression she applies her life coaching skills to empower women inspiring or established entrepreneurs/authorpreneurs looking to make an impact on the world.

Zaneta Varnado Johns is a three-time bestselling author of *Poetic Forecast, After the Rainbow, and Voices of the 21st Century* (2021 and 2022). She's a co-editor of the *Social Justice Inks* anthology. Her creative expressions appear in numerous international publications.

Art by Lisa Tomey-Zonneveld

Reflections

Thank you for spending your time with the
Garden of Neuro poets and artists.

We trust you enjoyed your journey.

If you would like to explore more about the

Garden of Neuro Institute, go to:

GardenofNeuro.com

GARDEN OF NEURO
INSTITUTE

www.ingramcontent.com/pod-product-compliance
Lightning Source LLC
LaVergne TN
LVHW022013080426
835513LV00009B/695